STRANGER

Also by Adam Clay

The Wash
A Hotel Lobby at the Edge of the World

STRANGER

poems by

ADAM CLAY

MILKWEED EDITIONS

Published 2016 by Milkweed Editions
Printed in the United States of America
Cover design by Mary Austin Speaker
Cover illustration by Mary Austin Speaker
Author photo by Jacques-Alain Finkeltroc

17 18 19 20 21   6 5 4 3 2
First Edition

Milkweed Editions, an independent nonprofit publisher, gratefully acknowledges sustaining support from the Jerome Foundation; the Lindquist & Vennum Foundation; the McKnight Foundation; the National Endowment for the Arts; the Target Foundation; and other generous contributions from foundations, corporations, and individuals. Also, this activity is made possible by the voters of Minnesota through a Minnesota State Arts Board Operating Support grant, thanks to a legislative appropriation from the arts and cultural heritage fund, and a grant from the Wells Fargo Foundation Minnesota. For a full listing of Milkweed Editions supporters, please visit milkweed.org.

Library of Congress Cataloging-in-Publication Data

Clay, Adam, 1978-
  [Poems. Selections]
  Stranger : poems / Adam Clay. -- First edition.
      pages ; cm
  ISBN 978-1-57131-463-5 (acid-free paper) -- ISBN 978-1-57131-909-8 (ebook)
  I. Title.
  PS3603.L385A6 2016
  811'.6--dc23
                                    2015017007

Milkweed Editions is committed to ecological stewardship. We strive to align our book production practices with this principle, and to reduce the impact of our operations in the environment. We are a member of the Green Press Initiative, a nonprofit coalition of publishers, manufacturers, and authors working to protect the world's endangered forests and conserve natural resources.

STRANGER

In the blue display of the cool cathode ray
I dream a highway back to you

GILLIAN WELCH

STRANGER

ONE

To Take Note of Where We Are

Plainly spoken, I am responding to you.
Despite our best efforts to will it shut,
the proof of the world's existence
can best be seen in its insistence,

in its opening up. Should we get lost,
let us be lost in a familiar space, surrounded
by every motion of the unnamed and unseen
until the moment they appear. With the sofa

in a slightly different place this morning,
the room resembles a dream of the room:
the details remain present and realistic
while everything bends toward one wall

in particular. I know what you want,
but the wind will not concern itself with us.

Northern Lights

Light or even a phrase or two
erased from the mind

like a once familiar street razed:
buildings destroyed, moved

elsewhere, tucked into the folds
of a tornado (you hope)—

One thinks many times not burdened by
but along with the clock—

Of course, it's a pleasure to arrive most anywhere

these days filled with desire
but once the mind's dwelling place becomes an ice cave

love defines its own tributaries with pine needles

or another way to say let's only speak
in the absolutes of morning, free of comparison,

of a drifting scale tipped to an almost perfect balance:

none of that language needed now
between meals, between the future departing from disaster,

and once the mind slows to the point of regression,

then what to make of the first memory arrived upon or within

for you what would it be and know
you cannot know what it would be for others—

Even in their telling
there's an orbit of masquerade around which no moon

could ever exist nor would it want to,
no perfect circle or symmetry to dwell within:

once the trees did not need their names and the night
needed no voice, it needed no knot

to unravel, it needed no one
to explain its madness to

Disruption Without Shrapnel

An admission of a river's deviation from whatever path
aligned to the stars, you clip a word from the mind

until it forms its own kind of mind:

a curtain meant to protect nothing, no castle of sky
creeping into view.

                        And what of the morning?

The newspaper troubles whatever glow
defined by the light.
                        Don't worry or wonder—

the world contains enough rubble
for the weight of every

body and for the weight of every body
we might imagine a space filled and emptied
again. In denying yourself

you deny a crucial part of the storm.

Along the Edge of a Season

Distant roads brought together
in a way described

as anything but pliant. Instead it seems

normalcy might suggest a stifled inspiration
destined to exist

as a hallway exists:

hidden between the rooms,
the Iowa of a house,

the Tuesday in a week with no Wednesday.

Somewhere a truck
does not turn over. It seems

there are no middles
anywhere—there are only

logical lists in sensible places.
Perhaps calling my view
of the world *palindromic* suggested

you wanted a window to work
both ways, that you
wanted coffee to put you to sleep.

Disregard the snowbanks in your mind.

Remember that ice expands
as it freezes—its memory doesn't

defer to urgency or to what
we desire. Snow

and legs keep moving through
the world listlessly. So much

for floorboards. So much for
absence that I once admired
or even desired as if

the world was in my shirt pocket
waiting to unfold

and scatter into the space between

the two of us. You suggested a shadow
could be musical

or that the neck of a giraffe mimics
the way some trees

stretch toward the sky,
free of knots and free of
the mark of history

upon them. It's easier to say

the word *quaint* than to be that way.
Was your attempt at sensibility
a worthy one? I don't know.

I don't know how to place the weight of a breath
behind the eyes. Money is a strange sort of memory:

remember the market with nothing for sale?
Remember how we corresponded

for a month straight with words
corrupted from their meanings?

An ashtray wasn't anymore.

Arbitration became so apparent
that suddenly knowledge (even a thought)
ceased to be incredible.

Take the words apart
and determine what a grin can be.

I'm not suggesting that grace deserves
a particular place in the world.

I'm suggesting that limitations
are rarely deserved by those

who impose them. Absence deserves
more. You said *waterlillies*
when I'm pretty sure you meant

something else, perhaps something
more distant. The sky was tinged

the color of a hangover that day,

and I knew better how to talk
to myself than to you. And then somehow

it's Tuesday again
and a school bus speeds down

our street between the parked cars
like some kind

of generous distraction from
whatever mundane thing
was hanging over everything else.

Maybe that word was *empire*? Perhaps
you were hoping or desiring

a bottle to place this house
(like a ship) into? I'm

hearing one thing
and speaking another. My
shirts aren't pressed. Hell,

they aren't even clean
and their colors
have run elsewhere.

In my mind, I see them bounce
on the laundry line

and wonder why.

I didn't understand what you meant

at the time, but it made sense
when I saw not a single bird in the woods.

The climate dissolved overnight
and you couldn't have been more disinterested.

A squelched fire hangs in the air
and in the memory

for years to come. It's a terrible thing
when we stop

and consider how having enough
means something

different from even a year ago. Think
of a swallow flying

from one tree to the next
and think of something from your own

life that runs parallel
to the experience of the first tree. There's
nothing. It's afternoon all of a sudden.

It's afternoon? If it is

it's a weird one, a place unfit for a poet
but not a place
unfit for other people

who calmly disregard
everything but winter
in a terrifying way. An idea

along the edge of a season
means much more. An idea

is one born from nothing
and destined to tunnel
its way into a hole meant
for a creature or for air seeking

out a place as only air does.

Overwhelmed? That's only half
of it. You can replace me
if you like. You can look

straight into a mirror and feel frantic all without me.
When I say *idea*, I mean *content*.

If you thought this was both the ending
and beginning of things,
you were wrong. It's all up

in the air, all past, future,

and present at once. One thing is certain:
we can't see past

speaking, and if we could,
it would only be a thread.

Don't Look Back

It isn't clear why one would want to see
the source of a river, but perhaps

stepping across the headwaters
amounts to something memorable.

This does not take into account

the fact that our memories only reflect
the moment we find ourselves in. Tomorrow

it's a distant sense of dread, but today
it's too normal for even

the news. Each day is a fit of beginnings,

and each day is determined to replace
the next. Too long we've been silent

on matters best left in the past,
and I keep forgetting each

righteous fact began as a trembling one.

Exhibit A

Would it be enough to suggest
the smoke from across the hill

suggests a type of life or a type of living?
I'd like to be stranger than I've been.

One bite taken from an apple and left
in the yard for an animal

to scavenge. Could this be a day
or any day? I'd like to think so.

I'd like to think there's something
to be said for closeness

to death, as if nearly leaving this world
can color our existence in a particular way

or another. *I miss you*, we might say
to ourselves in those moments,

but those moments lumber ahead
without us where another person

is making copies, sipping the last bit of coffee
for a day going,

a day already half-gone. *I miss you,*
we might say to each other in those moments,

as if repetition can be a way of
or even a minor attempt at remembering.

Home as a Haunt

Reconsidering or considering companionship seems

       too studious or perhaps
even too stubborn

for someone
as careful as yourself. This pathway

pardons care, but what you have
when you're all free of care
and gardens makes

as much sense
as where you began.

America's farmlands haunt your syntax,
your sense of being, or at least

the filter between an object and your notion of
       what it means

to exist as an object.

To be ablaze inside the color blue like a fixed identity
is to place a word

over here and another word there beneath
the first. This life maintains

its level of supposing so stoically
that you would think intention had given birth to it.

The End Time Before the End Time

Whatever an elegy's opposite might be,

the river outlasted the city
before this one,

old enough to know what should arrive
downstream and what should sink.

In anything's undoing,
we might imagine some notion of ourselves

but to what end does our mind direct us?

The throat manages its urges

for abandonment
with a mix of care and attention.

Like departing and arriving each morning
without much thought, luckily our bodies make

most decisions for us.

Even a Straight Line Must Curve to Shape the World

The fire it almost starts itself
Looks like water comes from somewhere else
—KURT WAGNER

My thoughts lost each day
in whatever linear pattern
appears at my disposal,
as if blaming the light
of noon for a midnight terror
wouldn't be nearly enough
recklessness for all or any
of us. On Short Street,
the steeples repair themselves
into a more fashionable
version of church: rhinestones
and glitter, retired pennies
cover all seeable spaces.
In my version of the future,
there's no need for disrepair,
no need for scaffolding,
no need for rerouting a river
up to the surface. Downtown
of yesterday and the stones
remain in the memory
like reminders of blocking
out the past. My mind
in these moments wants
to return to the linear, wants
to string a thread from here
to there in such a way that you
would think it had always
been there. At times here the seasons

feel fake, the summer's patience
only constructed for the sake
of violence and the sake of sustaining
our voices into the fluid corners
of night. Eventually terrorism
will look something like a truckload
of men driving through this quaint downtown,
plowing over parking meters,
resisting all attempts to monetize
what little open space we have left.
Of course our sense of terrorism will have
to adapt—perhaps even you will find
another use for your spare change?
Most things don't make sense
until they make sense—the birds
wash up in piles, their talons and beaks
the only evidence of what they
once were. In the next minute
you're skipping rocks across
the glass of a lake,
the sky so blue that ice
could fall right out of it.
No matter how hard I try,
I find myself returning back
to a logical way of organizing
everything, and I wonder
if I could recognize
madness in its current
river of form? A day on loan
can still be a type of day, the way
the light declines moment by moment,
and we witness the sky moving
away from the earth, a wreath of light
like a vision, like a weariness so divine.

Upper Peninsula

A bronze sky at first seemed the best way
to describe it,

but later the description

fell away into something
more vapid or mundane
than one might expect,

although the sky did not.
Your feet doubted the land.

Even a lawn chair

falling from the heavens
would have made more sense,

and even falling asleep while standing upright
felt more natural than this.

What we are is cut into the ground and continues

to burrow absentmindedly
into the source of our birth.

A shipwreck for every misguided

thought. A sandstone skipped across the water
ceases to dwell within

its boundary of definition. Do I

cast judgment on a song sputtering
out if I've never heard it before,

if I can't carry a tune in my head
or a fish on a line?

The sun parts the sky in a way
up here I never imagined

or learned it could. What's left
of the sky curves back around the lake

and a single spark from across the bay
stands in as something greater

than itself, I'm sure, but my
mind cannot trap

in its teeth. Certainly there's a better

way to say everything or anything—certain,
sideways, torn open,

and the fish I dropped from the line
(I dropped a thousand times now)

fries in a cast-iron skillet
on the gas stove while

the sour beer grows more
and more sour.

In your sleep a few weeks back,
you said you were dreaming and then you laughed

and rolled over and the street traffic

on the lower peninsula
continued, but the lake was the only noise

here and the linen closet opened
and closed on its own.

Someone in the woods hallelujahs
to the thought that the earth under us

is all carved out. It will make sense

to fill the place
where all that copper once was. Science dictates

the purpose of hollowness
and what air means

to the soil's underbelly. A grip, a grasp, a lock

of hair along the baseboard's chipped paint.

Like a building with its roof
taken off, distraction

becomes an inevitable disaster:
the snow piles up

along the walls, billowing
from the windows,

a pure form of pollution
if such a thing even exists

at this time of day, at this time of history.

And as our concept of history
changes under the influence

of wind and weather,
I become tied up in disregard

for most everything that the eye can see. This is all
wistful thinking, I admit.

This is all human nature has known all along,
but there are of course a million

ways to put a cliché to sleep.

The Northern Lights bookmark
the sky. It's certain

something in the air
or the wind will change us: the skin

cells end up elsewhere,
and we disappear into someone

completely different. I did not invent
the phenomenon

known as a marked tree. Disaster
was an imagination gone

wrong. Instead of living through
another, instead of years

falling into a leaf, our daughter outgrew the weeds
in the yard before we knew even her name

or where *even* ended and *odd* began.

A thought does not make water spring from a well.

Myths start somewhere:

the trees have always had limbs, the rivers
have always had mouths that spit a question
back at a question.

Our daughter grows like that very question:

she invents music,
sounds, words—water finds a way—and a bird

cannot be anything more
than itself anymore.

Our daughter grasps the ground
with her fist: the grass

goes with her, of course,
and what we are left with:

this little patch of space
to build a house. I did

not imagine that her birth
would require a whole new
vocabulary. I did not know

that fourteen lines would

not be enough to contain
what we knew was true

but were too ashamed to ask.
The cornfields open up,

the sun grows dull
in their glow, and the senses switch

places with each other. The floor
makes more sense

for sleeping at times—the bed
becomes a field after

a while, and language provides
a ground to stand on: the pine

exists because we call it that.
Necessity never needed us.

Pigeons fill a barrel—it might as well
be a sycamore to them.

There is no name
for the smell of the sap on the back

of your hand. There is only
the reinvention of light stitched

solidly to the night sky.

Sometimes I Miss Your Life More Than I Miss You

To learn a language or to marry
a form to another is without

guarantee or concern like a rock

in a snowstorm
depending upon your finding

it to exist. Time passes
strangely in every town

you enter, but what

if you do not
find yourself there?

How sudden the faces fall away

from your mind, from any mind
with so much upon it

and so much without it.
In most (if not all) instances,

the mind would prefer
to sleep and saddle the world.

Tell Me Now, Again, Who I Am

As if one instance of loneliness is unique
in light of all others, you allow one thought
to embrace the past, an absence of the mind,
although each shortcoming extends longer

in light of others. You allow thoughts
between moments to define what hunger means
although each shortcoming extends longer
as the meals grow further apart

between moments. Defining hunger
requires more than allegory?
As the meals grow further apart,
we find ourselves gone so easily,

requiring more than allegory
to allow past tense to become present.
We *do* find ourselves gone so easily:
the keys left all night in the door

allow past tense to become present
as if one instance of loneliness is unique,
the keys still left in the door,
embracing the past, an absence of the mind.

TWO

Start This Record Over

Perhaps is a new and sudden way of being.

Like satisfaction not yet begun or some other kind
of kindness:

a more gentle one?

Night makes us all into the middle
of something until we aren't

anything anymore. The sky
isn't any color here. It's OK
because consolation is color enough

for your cheeks, wind bitten and glorified
by the light of the wine in this glass draining

toward a better time, a better space. I invented
a notion of hell, and you invented a notion of hello.

Amazing similarities and bizarrely coincidental snow.

Like a twig falling from an oak's tallest point,

I keep wondering when forgiveness
found its way into this world

in a time before bargaining and beckoning.

It's quiet again and now the sky is a tangled
mess of rags seeking out the bored and unwilling.

I'd like to make a map not of the land
but of the path I took to arrive in this place,

a map with no idealized purpose,
a map of a thousand airless pines.

Sounds of an Emptying House

1.

A week or a month of images all clustered
around a single flower on a table

(on its way out)

does not intend to replace the sound

of a closet door closed
for the last time

or a moon framed by a ring held up to hold it.

In the background (with a stubborn weather burning off)
my mind reaches out reiterating

a solemn or solid unknowing—is this what
we've wanted all along or is this wanting

a symptom of *When what's lost has been found
and what's to come has already been?*

The light triggers a towering fear
and the forward-looking light manages

more than you or I can manage on our own.

On our own there's a way to be

that requires a smile opening up
into a laugh. There's a way

of forgetting unrecalled and tucked inside
your view of the world—I doubt I'd want to know

the world in that way or another.

If a southern state
ceased to exist, the purpose of our own being

would be something much more.

Not a day goes by that I don't think
about the rafter repaired
in the attic or the backyard sloping away

from the house in this manner or another.

Why bother with purposed distance or with distance
at all? Should forgiveness be such a believable
act that it would replace all other factors and factions

in the world? There's a way of stepping back
that someone now dead once taught me.

I'd rather maintain this view of the world.

Weather hidden inside each action
so strangely and in such an aware way

that only bread could be a believable miracle.

Are any miracles believable? Are you

(in your certainty) prepared for crossing a border
of this state on this side of the lake?

There's a way of asking questions
that begs the response

to be a non sequitur of noise
meant to be deeply detached

from even the parallel world it inhabits.
And in the word itself, why must

the word "habit" exist so solemnly and so quietly,
as though a memorial for your stolid existence?

You are a nonresident and I am a nonresident.

2.

I thought of and think of the house hollowing out slowly.

As it becomes larger, the ghosts that loom inside
grow smaller and become some sudden type

of music you once used to know all too well.
What would be if we didn't find the past coming back to us

so effortlessly? A peninsula mirrors more than itself

stretching out into the water. From up close
the house briefly misremembers each of its inhabitants

as solemn and regretful and exuberant

all at the same time.

                What if it could be just that simple?
What if all roads eventually fall away to dirt and gravel?

Most would if we would let them. Most ways of thinking

about the world exist in past tense and seem less personable
than the desire you once felt

for someone you didn't know

but wanted to. The distinction between a train
and a summer storm (on the first day of summer)

is so miniscule and so meaningless to even the most

observant outside observer. A highway here, a house there.
A forest where this tree used to be. Why must the ground

be so different in its silent regard for each battle

that happens above it? I thought forgiving each other
would somehow forgive the house as the walls moved

away from us. We left the stairway plaster
damaged as a way of moving on—those who replaced us

cannot understand and would never want to.

3.

How different can the touch of two people be?
Thankfully the days will grow shorter

from this point on—the simple idea of thankfulness transforms
into a gross imitation of itself.

I'd prefer it was more sudden or accurate

than this. I'd prefer a lot of things to a lot of nothing. When
    I came home
that next morning, the sheets were in the wash, and you had
    propped

the bed against the wall as if to suggest that the room
that day would be emptied too.

There are so many miles between this house
and that one. Each mile precociously maintains your sanity,
    a sanity

I could do without or care less for. At times—at night,
    especially—

I wish my honesty was blurred or smeared
with the desperate driven sky. Our daughter becomes aware

of metaphor in a way I never wanted. We should be better
    than this.

4.

Furniture feels out of context—

You said *no* in your sleep and then laughed.

We should be better than the emptying house that
was always eager to forgive whatever future might

occur within its walls. I keep thinking

of a long high hallway
somehow not large enough to contain

what it was meant to contain. At the end of that hallway
is just the memory of a ghost that seems

to look straight
through me

and then
straight through me.

What furniture is meant for a hallway? Or is a hallway

meant to only act as a passing through
or a passageway between two rooms?

Of those two rooms, I prefer neither. In transit

or in between
brings about its own strange silence

that buzzes so loud it becomes a sound all its own
that earns the gratitude of those who cannot feel grace.

Perhaps a structure should mean more than the objects that
    inhabit it.
Perhaps the cast-iron skillet left behind in the oven is the
    heaviest thing of all.

I keep thinking about that ghost.

A hallway is meant for hurrying
and for patience. If I could wake up early enough
I might see the sun rise,

but my eyes manage to be closed
most of the time—this means little more than what

it sounds like or what it might mean.

The ink stain on the wall
changes shapes into a memory

of a memory. Would your sense of necessity

tangle with mine if the world
was so untangled and hewn

with scarlet passives and missives?

Another cup of coffee
strung along this autobiography.

It's enough to acknowledge an emptying
until one empties along with the house,

the street, the city, the county, the state,
the country, the world. Belief

mourns just long enough and not long enough.

My perspective fails short of here—the horizon
seems to move near us, and I wonder if the lake

emptying is a possibility we might very well deserve

or earn if we face the other way for a thousand years
or if these thousand years will be our thousand years

and you will be standing in the field so sure of the plot
of land that the blue of your eyes will become some other color,

some foreign currency from a world that no longer exists,

a place no one could even want to exist, but our longing for it
remains the last thing we could possess.

5.

A stumbling through town (how many times did we?)
accomplishes what it intends.

6.

I'm not sure I can recall that town and those streets
even now. What is a week, really, in the scheme

of things? A polluted river and too much patience
does not lead to anything worthy or worth
our honest attention. If I were a betting man,

I'd bet on the river, but the town has been there
for a long time too.

There are ten thousand ways of looking at fate—
grateful for each one, I recall a million nights
when I avoided whatever missteps waited in the wings.

A list of similarities between this peninsula and that one:
exhaustive. Differences? The same.

An eagle seems to be enough currency for now.

Distance makes a dull memory,
and memory's wings prevent it from flying.

I hit a wall every hour on the hour.

A body of water is a body too large for the space of my mind.

7.

I doubt most things except for the eaves
of this moment. There's a way in which the world

seems to have contracted in the past that it will not in the
    future.

Like a conversation through a closed door,
there are better ways of going about these things.

If demanding closure is out of line,

then the line is traffic and traffic and then dust.
This house is full and temporary—

its sounds
slowly enter the mind in a few days,

and then the mind becomes a day
looking to either side for the past and future
as if reliance might as well be existence.

The basement burrows into the self even now
a week away from the house we left behind.

The kitchen manages to be even further away.

8.

In a house filled with furniture,
it takes little time

to pass through it
at night with your eyes closed.

When the house is empty
for the first time in years,

there's a stumbling on the first night.
The second night: nothing.

Perhaps there's no beginning worth beginning for—

The shadow of your face.

The face of the wall falling in toward me.

A beeline southbound
taking the better part of Vine with you.

The trees we planted in the front yard and the back
are now just trees, aren't they?

I realize there's something about bourbon
and the state further south—
the bottle's been aging since before this narrative began.

I don't want to be numb; I want
to understand numbness and carelessness.

I could fall right into the sand outside this house.

9.

I'm guessing the cranes will be around for a while.

There are certain things
that need not be brought into
an empty house.

I have already mentioned the sounds that persist
with such a gravity that they cancel one another out.

Does a piece of fruit rot from the inside out or from the
    outside in?

An abandoned puppet string or dental floss?

Some other things? I'd prefer not to catalogue
events as normal, mundane, or abnormal,

but for the sake of survival, we might as well
signal before changing lanes.

And then there's the kitchen:

the floor we walked
is the floor we put there.

10.

I keep thinking
of the body hidden

in each corner of the house,
but there's no sound—

most things muted
become loud enough

after some time.
A smile scatters

across the sky
above the house

like a flock of birds—
it's not a cloud

or a curtain of weather,
fortunately for us.

I wouldn't be surprised
if the roof of that house

was torn off within
the year—historically

speaking, it's possible
or permissible.

When was the last time
I slept well in that house

of trees? Curiously
I'm not sure and curiously

I'm forgiving myself
each morning in preparation

for the next day to come.

11.

It's disappointing the way we age together and apart
like the days which were meant to disassemble without us.

A violin is an old friend that dances
like we expect it to.

What an interesting
way of passing away

from houses with such speed.
There's another house,

a smaller one,
with a large yard meant

for more trees, but I'm
not yet convinced we will

plant them there.

Should we carpet

those stairs with such mindlessness
before we even inhabit

the space? Should a couplet
be enough for the time being?

The property lines intend to explain
what we own and what we don't

so succinctly.

12.

In a dream I was alive just long enough on this earth
to remind you of something you had always meant to do.

Whatever it was will remain
in the mind for a few more years

and it might have to wait until
the next life, a life we refuse

to prepare ourselves for. It always
comes back to the house and its soundlessness—

you refused

to pass through it one more time
and I keep passing through it

each night in the brief moments
of sleep next to you. The wind picks

up and turns a doorknob,
but we'd prefer it was someone

outside trying to get in,
and I wouldn't be surprised

if it was. I'm continuous
and a continent

of remorse, regret,
and calculated nonsense. It would be nice

if there were a word or two

in the house that I could just hear for a moment
or two. The kitchen sink drips

so certainly that I think it's raining outside
and then it's raining outside and the faucet
is only a memory. What does it take

to memorize a memory? A house

can change syntax in such a manner
that we assassinate most of our own attitudes

daily and wait for resurrections so surely
that we define the world with their occurrences.

These moments exhibit a disregard
for us and for our eternal unknowing.

There's a way of repairing
a house that makes it worse off

than it was before. Your laugh
enters the sky

not like a bird but like a single leaf
from the redbud that we waited to fall

through the month of October.
In my mind it's still there

and in your mind, there's no regret
for bringing the tree there

and walking away from it.

I keep dreaming of a wrecking ball
bringing the house

and its sounds to the ground
below the foundation

and into the basement we disregarded
for the better part of our quiet lives.

It's a perfect regret that I keep imagining
and then I realize there's no such thing

as a regret wished for or perfected
slowly through time
and through the wistful execution of the mind.

My face to your breast
could not be close enough to divorce

this moment from any others.

We left the curtains behind
and whatever was left in their folds.

A piece of glass from 1922.

My friend of a thousand beginnings,
a sound can only understand itself.

Not Quite Right

The trees without limbs
speak to you sullenly
for how else would
you expect them to speak?

A woodpecker gravitates
to the dead tree, solid
staccato through the rain
gutters, the snow melting

quickly. And as for the leaves,
we wait for their arrival,
the oak skeletons the sky
as we look up, waiting

for an ocean to discover us,
rocks blasted away
to sand in seconds, not
eons, not the weight of the moment

carved out of wood, laid out
in the yard for the worms without
movement, the birds with their
heads temporarily taken off.

Compost Hymn

A worm split in two
must be an ideogram for something.
Once someone said nothing
incomprehensible on earth can exist—

rather, one's vantage point
obscures understanding past
the point of sanity. Yes, this world
belongs to scavengers, and yes

we are briefly a part of it. This city
could be any city alive enough
to be mistaken for an elsewhere.
Often our linear notions are nothing

more than whims: the weather carries
this thought like a balloon to the clouds,
the lake below a memory
of a door boarded up from the inside.

Occupied Elsewhere

Should the mind go,

then it will find its way
in whatever speed

it will. Do not think
of a field colored to coal

with a thousand crows,
but rather

think of the single crow

in a harvested field
where corn once stood,

the prairie sky
like a disaster

yet to be named.
Your face was somewhere else.

I imagined no pantomime

of destruction: there was
only the fear of dissolving

or becoming a landscape
that never really existed,

a silo to contain each thought
surely made sense there.

Our Eternal Sounds

What might all songs lean into?

      You scramble eggs one moment,
and in the next minute

      you're eating them
with dry toast and black coffee

      in silence.

        On a day like any day,
your voice is not your own:

the grass clippings disrupt

a robin too large to fly
from worm to worm.

We don't know why we speak,

      but yet our voices
persist, even when void of substance—
          like a dream you'd like

  to recall throughout the day,

but you don't or you can't
and after a week, it's gone forever.

Of course our voices
evolve years before our bodies—

our vocal cords vibrate like a heartbeat,
        senselessly. No explanation
needed.

Eventually all languages converge.
        Each thought falls

into all others. And what thought
        resists being built by words?

                Perhaps fear placed us
        here in this room together:

a fear of fire at one point turned
into a fear of God. After that, a fear

of godlessness, a room
where a word before

        another word and another

word after the first
was all we had, all we could
imagine. Somehow

an image means
more than the object itself
but not because

        it's made of words. Most likely
it's because the act of creation

sets the mind down like a bird
      in a field

where the speed of the invasive cannot exist.

East Jackson Drive

                In a dream last night Kim
and I walked a few miles
                to a dry riverbed
                to see a tree where a poet

had died shortly after
                I was born, even though
                        in waking I know the poet
actually died in a house

                in Arkansas, a state I haven't
set foot in for several years
                now. As poets
                        all we can know
is that we are poets

                until a moment
and another and another

                manage to pass by without us
and without us knowing it. It was spring,
                        and the tree sat bare among

others filled with leaves. Snow fell, and I took
                her hand and one last look

at the tree, perhaps a meaningless artifact
                        in its lack
                of truth, the riverbed filling up with snow
and the snow filling up all around us.

The Cradle of All There Is

It had not been raining
that day or the day before,

although the forecast
was mostly grim most

of the time, as if the talk
of rain might keep it away

or at least harbor
a bit of hope for those

outside, such as a friend
I saw on campus

that morning, an acquaintance,
really, and we talked

briefly about the leaves,
the fires burning, and even

the way the days are named
by the glow of light

above their horizons, which
led me to ask her what she

was teaching that semester,
but she told me she wasn't

teaching, which was fortunate
because she had found out the day

before that she had cancer,
news that changed the name

of that day in such a way that
I didn't know where we were

or who we are. Of course,
I asked what we, my wife and I,

could do for her and she
told me *have another baby* in such

a way that it seemed like putting one
foot in front of the other or handing

the husk of a season to the next,
saying: *Here, this is yours*

because you will know better than I
what to do with it and what to call it.

Elegant Comparison

With the trees falling off the leaves,
the unworldliness

of the moment means less and less

until it means more and more, perhaps
like an undeserved term

of endearment
more deserved than the rest. How do you manage

to maintain such a smeared

poker face in the mind of what remains?
Most mirages exist,

urge us on, and then resist no longer.
Your stage left is not my stage left,

because we're in the business

of the overly obvious: like a past-tense
past due, like a squirrel in a trash can,
like a sensible sense of being.

Our Daily Becoming

Like animals moving daily
through the same open field,
it should be easier to distinguish
light from dark, fabrications

from memory, rain on a sliver
of grass from dew appearing
overnight. In these moments
of desperation, a sentence

serves as a halo, the moon
hidden so the stars eclipse
our daily becoming. You think
it should be easier to define

one's path, but with the clouds
gathering around our feet,
there's no sense in retracing
where we've been or where

your tired body will carry you.
Eventually the birds become
confused and inevitable. Even our
infinite knowledge of the forecast

might make us more vulnerable
than we would be in drawn-out
ignorance. To the sun
all weeds eventually rise up.

THREE

This Is a Frame

A poem is occurring every moment
for example
that fluttering of mute flies
-MARIO SANTIAGO PAPASQUIARO

Most mornings like this one,
silent and sudden, and then

you're awake
in a simple and dull sort

of beginning: the traffic
light along the edge of the couch

loud enough to mask
the intruding sun.

How to be noticed
in a world eager for absence,

eager for endless urging?

One's senselessness:
a surprise

like the sound of the newspaper landing
on the lawn, enough

for the birds of another year,
stopping over silently,

moving on. I don't like them,

I don't like the railroads,
the ambulances, the constant

noise of night worth little
less than its weight.

But what to do with the opposite
of nothingness? Can night

fill in the space
a sentence should?

You know what I mean:
the sometimes dull

collision of words
rolling around,
void of success or even

the temptation of it. Sometimes

I sing a sentence out loud,
then wonder if anything has escaped

my mouth. Today somehow
felt like the middle of something.

The roads gleamed up from the ground
and remained in the eye long after

they had been left behind. I rarely
hold anything in the mind

the way I held those roads.
Strangers waved

happily.
Neighbors looked up, as if

expecting just one traveler that day
and that traveler was me. Even

the cardinals and yellow finches
and flowers paused

in those windless moments. As I pass
through the house in the night,

I feel like an unwelcome stranger,
a traveler on the other side of the world,

a place no one looks up from,
where the insects

mistrust movement from a mile away.

It's startling how one's perspective
of self can morph
moment by moment into
another self altogether. The news

remains what it is,
the type of living only night can explain.

And as for framework?

We think of beginnings, like crawling
or rolling over into

the light. Sometimes my voice
boards the airplane before me,

exists free of the weight we all eventually
learn to regret and forget.

An attempt at weather borders the window,
and the window allows one's life

to pass more slowly than it should.

Like a horse track free of horses,
these days are a simple type of worry:

without a pause, we notice nothing. Without
nothing, the pauses precede

the notions we have of ourselves.

I speak
and then as if I've spoken,

you speak
and the walls echo the sound

back. I didn't mean to look down
on the seasons and their sense

of reality. Nothing could make
more sense than returning to boredom
like these moments.

Tomorrow scatters the wind
like a destructive force

of front matter. Our neighbors
move elsewhere—the sun

manages forgiveness
of the sky
or at least that's what its color

might suggest if a notion
could be accurate.

There's a pause
in imagining a thought
we have free

of each other.

If we can't sleep,
then why not?

If we can't allow the moments
to scare us back into our skin,

then what point is the skin,
its translucent vision?

I rattle off a date as if my memory

never went bad, as if the days return
the dust to myself in a saddlebag

of noise and revelry. These days
the flags stay

at half-mast. Why bother lowering
and raising the exasperating quotient?

I allow this beginning
as if there's a point

on the train platform in which none
of us will be able to

stay any longer. Some days
might feel like the strangest

song imaginable. No one's going
anywhere, but there's

a bit of joy hidden in inaction: like
laughing for the sake

of sadness. Or like swimming
in a river with no sense

of upstream. The weather takes
a turn for winter

deep into spring. I could see
my hand in front of my face,

and now I can't.
Somewhere another siren

in the night, another bed
unmade.

It's too easy to think of shapes
in an abstract

sense of the world:
soon all words

will evade definition,
senseworthy or not. The days

are worth waiting for,

a bite to eat, a meal to rush through.
Surely some moments of speech

burn upwards
in response to the sky, like sense

existing free of those who pause
long enough to notice it. Often

we don't imagine how or why
the world could be presenting

itself in such a fragmented manner.

I've lived here a long time, much
longer than two years. It's amazing
how the body can be so many places

at once. No one says I want to grow
up to stand on that train platform

on a Monday shortly before their
thirty-fifth birthday.

It's good no one
talks like that. To think of each
day as a peculiar one

would be lawful, merciful, holy,
inexact. There's something
to be said for perfection:

like a couplet, it's symmetrical
and certain. I've heard talk

of the sky today—it exceeds
even disastrous expectations. It's overtaught,
overconsidered. Its unfurling

becomes costly in these calmly
shredded moments. The trees manage

kindness toward one another. One along
Broadway and Third
was split open. Penny

asks what happened to it,
then asks

if we can live

inside of its broken trunk. I suppose
any question one might ask

could be surrounded or surprised
by the innocence implicit in it.
Strangely enough,

solitude can be a kind of currency,
like the way the clouds

disrupt the sky with their tiny
rafts void of color,

soundlessly. At times when
driving through the countryside,
I'm amazed at how few

flowers I can name. And then
I think of the trees as if I'm not the only one
passing through this world,

no words

fit for my mouth. As if tornados
only exist in August, you wonder

what month it might be right now.
We lie on the grass

and consider the sky
from a low vantage point.

Now I pause,
think the news is unbelievable

and it is.

Soon it's raining when
it ought not to be:

the clouds grit their teeth,
the newspaper ends up
down the street, in a drainage

ditch. The aisles we follow

blur into blue.
And what else is meant
aside from the exploding pops of sky

reflected in the eye of a child?
I wish a sonnet could contain
any day in its perfect grip.

I marvel at the joy of containment—

what won't fit simply ceases to exist.
Idealized or boiled down to a simple nod

toward the dark side street
of whatever town you happen

to find yourself in. It's a small life
we have on our own, some think. Others don't

bother processing even the dull fact of morning.
Where do you

fit in? Like an outdated catalogue,
a season reaching past its climb?

For weeks, it seems, you've
memorized the patterns of each day,

as if the act
might remove you from the passivity
of supposing, not enough
cloud-cover

for the daylight hours left. Like our bodies
closer to each other, merging

into a single voice, the parting
puzzles us even more. Language

never transparent enough for me:
hidden by syntax, the meaning

of a word lost,

tucked into the folds
of the earth. I spent

hours interrogating
the sentences I thought

before I spoke them. Inside my head,
there's a lack of sense,

which I know
you already know,
but saying it makes it as real
as the headlights cutting

through a bedroom night.

Who could believe or stand by
what ideas

they promise? In birth,
we're assuring a future

worth existing in and for.
The doors lock

surely. The thought
of a cloud,

maybe some grass washed

down into the sewers. We don't
care what the city

might think. In fact,
we don't

think a city
exists, like borders

and their organization
is fumbling enough for a day

we remember, forget again.
Like a song from another time,
we are free of ourselves,

of what our arms
trace and retrace. If my sense

of love is worth a life outside
my own, then

these moments are worth
themselves or more.

Growing tired,
the days yawn toward us,

wonder how long we'll persist
recalling one single thing;

I recall another memory
altogether. Would the melding
of the two somehow be reality
exacted, as if our memories

are two separate sentences snaking
through each other? There's little

to say in observing consumption:

we might as well
not be there.

The sky can seem insanely unreal
so we laugh until

the inside of our laugh is a deep mistrust
of the disturbing things

we do.
Are you OK

with missing a meal
for the sake of the rocks and their calling?

What are you outrunning?

Now the light grows less casual,
more ominous. Patchy frost

in the forecast is such a minor
disturbance,
the memory of where

one might have stood,
the way the grass was cut

it might have been a painting. The dullness
of perfection at times is desirable:

just imagine a cup of tea

or bourbon or coffee,
and it's there in your hands

so suddenly that your awareness
almost makes you spill it. And the

dirt holds
more than you'd like

to think, or that's what the glance
of a stranger might suggest:

the sky an inkblot of nonsense:
most holidays

are forgivable long enough
if they disappear for even longer

than the time they take. It's easy
to imagine another outcome

running recklessly through
the night, and soon

there's a mirror for each
thought. An object

looked at this way:
does it depend

on the point in which it enters?
In which it forgets it was

discovered? The grass green:
I know the rain won't

last, the long summer
isn't far off. But

I try to capture it
like an idiot, like

bait lost in the waves,
but further back

into the land, the river crosses
a city of questions:

the skies earn their color,
the quilt you made floats off

into the air.
When you think of a piano,

I know you think of a swamp
meant for holding back the land: the dry

skin, the lamplight
from your bedside table,
a desirable blurring

and a blurring that boredom
slips its knot through. The only residents

here are upstaged
by the soil: recollection

becomes a fragment of itself:
likeable, laughable,
hindsight from the back of a horse

looking toward the straight line the horizon
promises. And what

then? What will music maintain
when language cannot? Sometimes

I imagine departing
for that stretch of trees,

a single book
or two could be enough.

The fireflies refuse
this late season:

abandoned pockets
and the curtains drawn

against the breeze
and the way it floods
an acre.

The way a sentence can fall apart
in your hands is a wonderful thing.

There's more than one way
to take the world apart:
either way, outcomes

believe in our actions: the blackbirds
all fly away but one:

the morning remains well
through the afternoon,

and the flags are nowhere
near half-mast. They catch the birds

in their unfolding,
they release them to the sky.

And what worth assigned to the stars
in the blue of day?

Were we to part the trees
and find an ocean,

would we be more surprised
than we find ourselves

now? We drive toward
a point on the map
and the time takes

us too—slowly, there's
a beginning at play.

You are the entire state,
a hand. No one knows

the source of illumination,
but we accept the light in the same way

we accept each day: with weariness and worry.
The salvaged detonators ended up

elsewhere. But what if they had stayed
in the same place? Would anyone have feigned

surprise? Thunder struck, and Penny
thought it was a volcano, though
it was a miracle

it wasn't. I hear the lakes

are still frozen in Minnesota,
and the mosquitos in Louisiana

block out your vision when they fly by.
It makes sense

when repetition doesn't. It won't be long
before the streetlights

become a luxury, how many
gallons of water used how many times

a day? The gutted apartment
buildings unnerve me enough,

but it's momentary
and not before sleep. What

kept you awake last night
or has your memory

been eclipsed by the exhaustion
of the dandelions? You don't

need to be hill bound to know
how a city can empty

out slowly until it's mistaken
for heaven. Before the days

are built, they're before us:
a party no one's

invited to. And lights
we fumble toward are forgotten

more easily than recollection: rain,
no rain, steampipes filled

with steam. After a while everyone's
wearing a suit and the doors

seem to open by themselves. Boredom
like a black bird

roosts heavily on the branches
of this tree.

You get your hair cut
in your sleep: the rain runs backward

to the sky, and the rivers
mirror constantly. I suppose

we could visit some faraway
place, see the inside of a temple,

avoid the civil war happening
at that moment.

Noise I do not
understand, but I'm trying

to. And as for other explanations
of nonsense, we close

our eyes to the clouds,
but they remain there: the rain, though,

is elsewhere and our minds
go there too. I love

how even
free of retribution we wonder

if we should
give thanks to something or someone

for the endless ebb
and slowness of days.

Here in the bluegrass,
I'd like to catch a train to downtown

Versailles and sit outside on a street corner
and wait for you

in that blue dress
to walk by. I guess most everything

is the translation of something else:
I keep track of words,

ideas, without knowing origin.

Why bother with notations meant for skywriting?

Remember the parade that happened
for no good reason? Remember the stars

that seemed to hang below the sky? We kept
going for walks, not meaning to. The walks
took us with them

and with enough silence,
the ants ceased
noticing us. I suppose

there are words
for what this feels like:
a life never to be. I'd be lying

outside if I had enough sense,
but my dreams have mistaken

me for someone else. I'd like

to plant a seed in the ground
and stay awake to watch

it grow up through the soil
and bloom

into something worth remembering.
Sure we sleep well
for a few hours, dodging

night the only way
we know. What

did you say you loved
before the grass growing

along the edge of that hill over there?

The impression
I was under was that it would

be less sudden, more like water
rising slowly up to the back door
over the course of a dozen years

while you watch out front
for any sign of change. Some days

I walk away from words
and when I return,

it's strange to think
where the mind's gone:

the humidity no longer
hides in the full trees;

it triggers the memory
of a stranger's face or the solitude

of a morning stolen away
and forgotten just long enough.
There's probably
a reason the way we imagine

ourselves will dissolve slowly.
In these days

grace doesn't have a home:
look how clumsily I unload
the dishwasher, mop the floors,

take the trash out through the mud.
Fireworks in March

for no good reason, though
maybe my mind

has mixed the months:
it's all one day happening

like a conundrum
of a dream, the engine

falling right out of a car.

Should listening take the place

of movement, the wind
will evolve into an elsewhere.

Daily, there's a self-imposed

exile, but it's never been clear
what you're separating yourself

from. Like the route you drive
each day could make a difference.

Like running into a thunderstorm,

sand and glass blowing into your

eyes, would deliver
you from deliverance.

At some point
syntax falls away from the idea

it once attempted to contain.
There was a time before

we said much of anything
worth much,
but it was a quality
in one another

we both admired so gravely

that we continued on
so as to remain

idealized in the minds
of one another
and those who happened

to stumble into
our patient unfolding.

Over time, this silence
became its own

type of language. I paid
attention to detail

in such a debilitating
way that the world

would not disappear—
nothing could

cease its existence, even
if my memory of the object

died in the night.

I told you these things
and more,
certain words
as easy as breathing,

and breathing complicates
the living we do between.

Each breath
I've known has opened

over time—refusing
to do so would simply

mean a disconnection
of sorts. The river makes the trees

sway and the swaying
is a type of forgetting. Suppose

toying with memory
is all life really is?

It's amazing
how even the most basic

thought can paralyze
a day, the bats
flying overhead at dusk,

and we have faith
in their return,

all the stops
and starts as if the days

provide some kind of logical
notion of night. Some days,

the flowers descend from the sky
around us; their desire

to touch the ground might
be masterful if it wasn't

so terrifying: we blink

and something else is gone,
something else arrives. I walk

out into the front yard, bourbon
in hand, and find silence

in each footprint of grass,
fire prepared but never lit.

Our daughter set a tiny table

for dinner; I sat crowded in a seat
meant for her, wondering what

had happened up until that moment
to bring me there. The nights are filled

with apples: I take one from the fridge
when I can't sleep, pace between

the rooms slowly, looking for something,
though I know deep down inside

there's nothing I'm really looking for;
I miss the child in my arms,

the birds insane
with beauty.

Tomorrow's Decoration Day
and in silence we mourn

more than we wish to:
the birds that don't return,

the airplane that skitters
the runway, the ocean

retreating from itself. How a room
can change depending

on light isn't a conversation
worth having.

Or should we
gather up sticks, build

a fire, and hope to

see ourselves in it? It should
be easier to define the days

by the lack of light, the silence
of the streets in the morning

on a holiday, nowhere
for breakfast, nowhere open

to patch a flat tire or patch
the sky

into a quilt worth

remembering. This town
exists without fire

escapes, without fires
most of the time,

though sometimes the sunrise
is as catastrophic

as catastrophe can be. I don't
want to mistake

the news
for the news,

but blame me from whatever
perspective you'd like to

take. Plate covers

off the light switches,
the paint drying slowly

in the dull heat of late May.
My mistakes could

be anyone's but who among
us has a guide

that's not filled with drastic
measures, moon-heavy phrases?

One has to pause at the end
of anything and wonder
to keep from losing the mind.

The doors do not lock
or are not locked,

as certain as uncertainty:
the paragraph is too tidy

to contain the mess left
behind: continue

grouping, organizing,
remembering,

and forgetting, should we?
Or should we devise a new path

through a familiar place of
forgetting,

one you knew in dreams

well enough? Words aren't
enough. A phrase isn't

either, but the space
a body holds in any moment

is a marker of something greater
than ourselves.

The streets we take
all point westward,

and there's an allowance
I'm getting used to,

accepting, and slowly
learning I won't understand.

In the day
we can reinvent

sound with such ease
that the world becomes

curtained,
riverbanks filled

with songs and sand.
Another bridge

falls into another river,

yet along the peripheral vision
of a child

there are no words
yet for the things
she sees, though the images

maintain their own heaviness:
a cemetery filled

with golden light,

the flowers growing less sure
of themselves in the wind,

and the rain as the sun sets
and rises in a city collecting noise.

FOUR

Abstract Evolution

My daughter with enough mysticism
for us all, an obscene building
drifting up from this main street filled

with a mania no one will bother to name,
for naming might as well be a flood
of mirrors, a crack in the mind we'd rather

not concede. No point in paragraphing.
No point in boxes born from the mind's
darkest points, although train tunnels

a simpler shade of black spill
from the mouths of most animals
(even in daylight), an odd form of money

but not a place to begin. For this we do not
pay a price. I do not know if it is the mind
that gives shape to the world.

For the First Fog of October

If an idea exists but is never found,
then the stained-glass windows

will reflect nothing back to the ear.
Most days filter through the mind,

waiting not for movement
but for a road to be built,

brick by brick, word by word,

weariness replaced with joy,
but what is joy without the years

and the way they open constantly,
two or three hearts pumping a volume of blood

meant for just one?

           Our disbelief in the ordinary
emerges from the way we color routine:

leaves pile up depending on the wind,
but why pause to notice?

Eventually the seasons embrace
what our words will not, the illuminated day

just one of a thousand others,
and the names we give back to the world

mean ultimately little against the way

the sun pleads sense
from the smallest cradle of dew.

Glare

There's somewhere a city, but the bridge
of our understanding derives
its presence for only

so far and connects little worth reporting.
We go about finding some books about cities,
old ones with piles of ash

and broken vases and barely half a smidgen
of knowledge about what their inhabitants
ate when life allowed a pause

or two. In choosing
not to document, we are deciding
we *should* document

like a path we take to work
emerging from a cocoon of meaningfulness.
We'd like to glare tragedies in the light

of disappointment and invite the first moment
you open your eyes in the morning to stay
around for a while, the birds burrowing

their boredom into the unbroken branches
of the trees that run between loneliness
and nirvana, the mercy for which no words exist.

Season

Niedecker says
In summer silence moves

and that seems
about right

or right enough
for blurring

the lines of this
coffee not

cold enough yet.
I can still feel

the miles of road
from last week,

the movement
of months. In

the backyard,
a strip of grass

cut, the rest tangled
up to the sky,

a path for the helicopter,
no, a paper

lantern, to follow.

Honest Attempt

Perhaps geography is a casual
attempt at knowing
the volume in a glass, the fragments

of paper lining your pockets.
Our ancestors remain our ancestors—
they've come before us draining

the boards from the boardwalks,
the elevators from their cables.
If all inventions are born from

necessity, then what need
explains why we are here?
I used to know this countryside

and the creak of every
house I've lived in. In reflective
reflections, there are mountains,

there are rivers, and at least
one single sea. The symmetry
that defines and comprises

our faces is certain, everlasting,
senseless. I suppose this is why
questions exist and why a cluster

of days, all added up, amount to
a single memory, recalled so many
times it's not even itself anymore,

not even a pathway to knowing
who we once were, like a pile of leaves
blown away in the movement of night.

First Winter in Kentucky

1.

For what does it truly mean to fear water
turned into ice (or turning,

as the water along this town now is)?

                Today the world grows
more and more devoid of chance

or even luck with the birds moving deeply away
from the landscape they've inhabited for so long,
entirely unaware of their own uncertainty.

The days once opened like a canvas
and closed around the memory

of themselves so perfectly, driven
toward the day bound to follow.

I refused to call
               even a shadow dreary,
chasing thought after thought
from my mind

because there has always been
an after all-ness to oblivion that I've found attractive,

if only for the way it dulled the mornings
into a stubborn afternoon

engrained in jewels of regret
and mournfulness. I keep considering a step back

from this season toward the past—isn't this
what we do best? But the light of day

has been the only gospel
I can derive from anything tangible.

And what to think, really, of tangibility
amidst these fields used to holding

so much snow the rivers would rather forget?

Truly, I'd prefer not to replace
a moment with another—a house
is such a sullen and inappropriate

metaphor because under the surface exists
a way of being built. Walk

to one side of the room and the light shifts
with your movement (or with the moment)

and toward your own sense of headway.

What it's worth
or the idea of what it's worth

believing movement is for
somehow drifts up

to the mind this time of year
like the name of an apple

I fully expect to forget, recall, and forget again.

I like managing these moments.

These moments set sail on text meant for only a month ago—

2.

The sun as a dart. The sun managing
its consistency even here.

I'd be lying to say pictures
of the dead don't
provide their own type of comfort.

Toting the compost bucket
out into the yard is a brief way of being,

if only for its manner of becoming

or its manner of believing, something
the limestone rivers shrink away from
and the days shudder toward—

3.

Hilly, no mountains, with a rag of a morning
tied around your neck

so perfectly and so slowly for why

must details bring so much

hesitation with them and their
singing? The days splinter

into themselves, away from themselves
it's snowing   it's raining

and fortunately the fields resist a word
in the shape they're in. Your gladness

for being here sometimes washes
away with the slowly
turning scrap of land we would never

believe in had we only read about it haphazardly
before bed and after a glass or two of something

too strong for the blood that could fill this room
or town better than a sigh of light.

Bourbon and rye—

boredom. A beginning might
as well be deepening trouble—just tack a name

onto a name and onto another. When we are born,
we are who we are. It's just managing or an undying
resistance against the inevitable

that makes us the person others see us—and will see us—as.

I can't determine whether I'm standing
close enough to this fact

to make sense of it, looking from the angle of an angel
as if to destroy meaning and music at the same time.

4.

A small place to live in—

"Quail and Dumplings" skitters through the room.

A sea certainly might have the best of intentions.

5.

For this moment:

the walls painted red do more than needed,
although noticing would require

needfulness beyond repair. To find my way around

might require more, too, than I've been compelled
into or beyond. Should bolstering

light be an occupation? Should an occupation
even damage a winter day in such

a frame of mind or in such a way
that we think of elsewhereness

before we think of a place meant
to hold up an infinite number of moments?

Don't bother defining effort
or the urge felt with such a sense of greed

that you submerge it into the tired folds
of your memory and the space

your memory fills. It's a good day
for a thousand regretful motions,

but not one of them will be enough or good enough

or manageable enough to string ourselves around.
Everything happens on a surface,

but surface level rarely makes room for a surfacing.

6.

This morning's nothing more than fragments
of a leftover matinee: purposeful

but unreasonable. The morning has a way of creating
its own space before we're too sure to notice

it's even there. A minute goes by in love with the next—

I never knew why I'd think of this exchange, this transfer,
as a promise made good, but I did. Was it a blatant

indication of what's at the core of you and I?
Winter remains, yet the air outside says otherwise,

the weather disregarding our patterns so exactly
we know it was here long before these patterns ever emerged.

7.

I'd like to maintain a consistent voice

or maybe I'd like to maintain a consistent
direction to cast my voice in—in some sense

it's all the same—

the sky strung with lights all shot out:
the manner of being, a new way of seeing.

8.

At the turn of the year I don't know why,

but we pause and stop to consider the reasoning
for most everything.

I'm too certain
that the folds of a year

can subsist independent

of the thoughts as they collect
all around. The straw spun

along the highway's edge
takes the place of snow, and I count

each exposed nest garnered in the trees,
because losing count

might be what I do best, all things considered
and all things inconsiderately golden.

There's a way of saying goodbye
a curtain can say less of.

When this is what winter
looks like, winter is what's loved best.

9.

The punch line: nothing can go wrong
if nothing exists. If winter

never occurs, then can a summer exist

or, worse, would it persist? I imagine a letter worded

so perfectly and left on top of the snow momentarily
before being covered up by more snow.

A word might melt away like the rest of us.
The combination of words

might be only part of the whole and maybe even
a smaller part of themselves. The sun

through these clouds is a cup of coffee

as viewed from above. I don't want
to think about what this says I am or might ever be

because for now I see so many birds in the sky,
they look like the most urgent horizon of all—

Nightcap

Some mornings I read poems
and my first impulse is to remain silent,

as if even the simple act

of conversing would further complicate
a world continually unfolding before us.

Perhaps like an observer on the outside of a field,
perhaps like an observer on the outside of a field,
the field has somehow clouded the space around me.

In moments like last night, one can't help but wonder
about the sharp edge of a year and the dullness

of them adding up, one by one. It's certain
I'm not the same person I was back then and even now
I have a temptation to swerve this life off

into another one. If life is a flight
where *I lose everything and everything belongs to oblivion*
then I can live with that. After all, what choice

do we have? An observer on the outside of a field,

I am a different person altogether.

I am suddenly standing
there with you, your hand touching my arm.

The Hardness and the Brightness

As memory blurs
to the point of clarity,

the wind provides
occasional marked moments

like this one:
aging grown ageless—

you see a tree
in every stage of being.

It only takes a breath
to see what cannot

be defined by words.
Of course this bed

could be any bed in
any city in any state,

but why must you
connect what demands

departure? The mind
imagines disunion so

dumbly, so openly, it
might be a way of surviving,

like a snowplow to the infinite
islands of straw and thistle.

Everyone Trying to Start / Something New

I realize: what words we manage
are only as useful as how

the words manage to use us.
In the gnarls and twists of the world

and the twist of our lives alongside
the eaves of these moments,

I realize there are few things to say
for a day as heavy as this one: twenty children

taken away in Connecticut,
a dear friend gone in Denver. These days

remind me *I'm allowed to be a human again,*
and that everything is dialogue until it isn't

—and there are stories, flashes of poetry,
and a nightcap those

of us still here to remember are thankful
to have had. Of course, in the near and far away

we all wonder what we will wonder,
but this wonder allows me to drift

unapologetically—and perhaps thankfully—
into the gaze of sentimentality

when I think of how these losses
are all reminders of a sort: every record

flipped to its B side is only grace
garnered with more grace.

On Silence and Sleep

The days remain themselves
from this vantage point,

a curtain drawn around a world
void of sense just long enough

to be logical. I don't recall those
first moments we spoke,

the weather, or what conflict

could have been occurring
in the neighborhoods

carved out around us, its developments

somehow the best indication
of repression even in the sober light

of the world's sway. At times,
I begin to imagine

conversations before they happen, car accidents
occurring a thousand miles away,

or a building being
built before its foundation

is even imagined.
All of this is to say or explain

my tendency toward silence
even if your stance

remains unexplained for the time being,
something I mull over, consider, accept.

When I wake up each morning,
I think of the day that Hopkins

encountered: one darker than night,
one filled with gall and heartburn,

an ocean of oceans fumbling
in and over and through the mind.

And what does this reveal about one's thoughts,
or could it be the same for all of us?

I know there are those who wake up at peace,
rested, quietly considering

the life of a day and how to live it.

There are those who don't sleep at all
for fear of never waking up.

And then there are those so young
they've yet to have their minds directed

toward either possibility,

although it's only a matter of time before
it happens, which we have to accept, too.

A nightmare woke Penny
last night, her head buried

under her blanket when I went
in to console her

and bring her to bed with us. And then
this morning, I woke before her,

memorized her face

in the gray morning light, her mouth moving
in sleep as though—or because—

another life was happening there.

This Pastoral Way of Living

To break a season open
with your bare hands

would mean disregarding
our own perceptions
by replacing them

with the obsessions of others.

In light, the world exists
through our knowledge
of the sky, tree limbs,

and all types of weather,
as if anything could fall,
as if anything

could be categorized so simply

as either weightless
or disruptive.

I step over raised dirt
most days, pretend

that its existence can be its own type
of belonging.

The trees do not move
unless the earth thinks to release them.

Should we be envious of their immobility?

Would it be sensible to pause daily
in a sense of knowledge or fear?

And what else?

I don't entirely believe that one
must see something

to understand it.

In Kentucky, there are horses
everywhere, and there are hundreds

of roads you can take to see them.

I believe in the pastoral
because I live in the pastoral,

the trees are so bucolic

here they call out at the end of the day,
bent under the weight of our unknowing.

Some days I take the dogs out to run at land

once owned
by the Boone family—there I watch

the blades of grass stir, and I pause to think

about the complications language
can bring into the world, a world

we can lie down in, a world where often
the horses disregard our presence.

Like a double fence along the highway,
the mind is an expanse, although

there's always an end, a border. From
one thought to another, I'm calling out to you,

I'm calling out to you,

as if we're building a nest, one word at a time.

Forecast and Its Failure

Penny collecting rocks from the shore each day,
a pile on the piano bench, some underfoot,
others disrupting the smooth rhythm of the kitchen table:
flint, quartz, basalt, sea glass, chert.

Moments become disallowed from memory:
the shallows of the day like the shadows of the day.

While she sleeps, we return the rocks to water,
as if the negation of a moment also admits its existence.

Each day begins with a rock in the palm—
the lake exists to saddle our apology.

This poem was not erased from another.

Here, life mirrors what we can't quite speak.
Our skin seems too alive to hold us in.

Trading in a wishbone for a branch,
broth boiling on the woodstove,
a family of loons circled from above,
sand making the water deeper than it should be,
a hummingbird too big to be a hummingbird.

Biographical Patterns

Something to be said of kindness

like a bridge
where no water should be
or fumbling into the streets,

shoes tied together,

trash cans knocked over,
and a strange color of ownership
the sky has turned.

Don't write
like this is your *Selected Poems*—
there's enough nonsense

to go around
believing in with or without

a clouded perception
and a derailed train for each of us,

an infinite number of radio stations
hidden in the sharp static of pain.

I'm going to walk around the block
you think

even though there's a fence
back there and the snow

has turned
back into rain

as forecasted. There's
something familiar about your

type of undoing that's admirable
but what's admirable isn't always

a point driven all that well,

because even some
moments lack

the glory you imagined
them having in the mind.

There's always at least one
glass of water

left behind in the house,
a simple reminder

of your mind's mortality,
the synapses connecting

here and there not
as well as they once did.

Music somewhere,
a dog barking

through an injury. Believe
me when I say

I'd rather not piece

together the past in fragments: it's

a line arcing into the sky

at the moment I expect
it to. Remember
what those before
us asked we do:

whatever
we have to think,

think it well.

What I Remember

Even our resting bodies
will not illuminate

the rooms of our childhood.
Where did what I

remember go?
My daughter's hands

manage to be little
knives in each of her

delicate urgings.
Look how even

the sky drifts down
to tiny shreds

of light. Look
how I see myself

growing wiser
the less I learn.

NOTES

"Along the Edge of a Season" owes much to Paul Killebrew's "John Fucking Ashbery" from his collection *Flowers*.

"Exhibit A" and "Everyone Trying To Start / Something New" are both for Jake Adam York. The latter takes its title from his poem "Radiotherapy" and the italicized line is from an e-mail from York on June 2, 2009.

"Tell Me Now, Again, Who I Am" takes its title from Ted Berrigan's "Sonnet XXXIV."

"Sounds of an Emptying House" uses lines from Bob Dylan's "Pressing On."

"East Jackson Drive" was written with Frank Stanford in mind.

"The Cradle of All There Is" takes its title from Mary Ruefle's "After a Rain."

The opening line of "Elegant Comparison" was borrowed from Penny Clay.

"Nightcap" was written after reading Bob Hicok's "Equine Aubade" somewhere between Stillwater, Oklahoma, and Denton, Texas. The poem also includes a line from Jorge Luis Borges's "Borges and I."

"The Hardness and the Brightness" takes its title from Philip Larkin's "Sad Steps."

ACKNOWLEDGMENTS

Thank you to the editors of the following journals and magazines where earlier versions of these poems appeared: *BOAAT*; *Cimarron Review*; *Columbia Poetry Review*; *Crab Orchard Review*; *CutBank*; *Dark Sky Magazine*; *Descant*; *Forklift, Ohio*; *Fou*; *iO: A Journal of New American Poetry*; *Kenyon Review Online*; *The Laurel Review*; *N/A*; *Octopus Magazine*; *Phoebe*; *The Pinch*; *Southern Humanities Review*; *Toad Suck Review*; *Tupelo Quarterly*; *The Tusculum Review*; *The Volta*; and *Waxwing*.

"Forecast and Its Failure" was published as a broadside designed by Gina Alvarez in conjunction with the Fort Gondo Poetry Series.

"Our Daily Becoming" was originally published July 9, 2014, at the *Poem-a-Day* project of the Academy of American Poets, and also appeared in *Poem-a-Day: 365 Poems for Every Occasion* (Abrams Image, 2015).

This book would not have been possible without the generosity of so many dear friends and readers: Michael Robins, Ada Limón, Matthew Henriksen, Shannon Jonas, Alex Lemon, Kate and Max Greenstreet, Beth Marzoni, Rachel Swearingen, Juliet Patterson, Rachel Moritz, Mark Turcotte, Paige Webb, Mary Austin Speaker, Casey Patrick, Allison Wigen, Elizabeth Ireland, and Joy Katz. I also owe much to the amazing Milkweed Editions family: Daniel Slager, Patrick Thomas, Connor Lane, Joey McGarvey, Stuart Pease, Casey O'Neil, Kate Strickland, and Abby Travis.

And as always thank you especially to Kimberley and Penny.

ADAM CLAY is the author of *A Hotel Lobby at the Edge of the World* (Milkweed Editions, 2012) and *The Wash* (Free Verse Editions, 2006). His poems have appeared in *Boston Review, Ploughshares*, and *Crab Orchard Review*, and online at Poetry Daily and the *Poem-a-Day* project of the Academy of American Poets. He coedits *Typo Magazine*, serves as a book review editor for *Kenyon Review*, and teaches at the University of Illinois Springfield.

milkweed
editions

Founded as a nonprofit organization in 1980,
Milkweed Editions is an independent
publisher. Our mission is to identify, nurture
and publish transformative literature, and
build an engaged community around it.

milkweed.org

Book design & typesetting by Mary Austin Speaker
Typeset in Stempel Garamond

CPSIA information can be obtained
at www.ICGtesting.com
Printed in the USA
LVOW10s0538190518
577769LV00001B/41/P